The
Marble
Book

The Marble Book

by Richie Chevat
Photographs by Martha Cooper

Workman Publishing
New York

Library of Congress Cataloging-in-Publication Data
Chevat, Richie
    The marble book/by Richie Chevat: Photographs by Martha
Cooper.
    P. Cm.
    Includes indexes.
    Summary: Provides information about the history of marbles,
different types, collecting them, and instructions for many
games played with marbles.
    ISBN 0-7611-0449-6
    1. Marbles (Game)—juvenile literature. [1. Marbles (Game)]
I. Cooper, Martha, ill. II. Title.
    GV1213.C43 1996   96-604
    796.2—dc20   CIP
                                                 AC

Workman books are available at special discounts when
purchased in bulk for premiums and sales promotions as well as
for fundraising or educational use. Special editions can also be
created to specification. For details, contact the special sales
director at the address below.

Workman Publishing Company, Inc.
708 Broadway, New York, NY 10003-9555

Manufactured in the United States of America
First printing April 1996

10 9 8 7 6

Table of Contents

CHAPTER 5

Introduction

"What? Have you lost your marbles?"

There, we got that out of the way first thing. Naturally, when you tell people you're writing a book about marbles, that's what they all say. Let me tell you—after hearing it 300 times, it's not so funny. So let's get this straight right now—that's the last time you will see the words "lose your marbles" in this book. Well, actually, that was the last time, but really, that's it!

This book is about marbles—playing marbles, collecting marbles, the names and types of marbles, famous marble players, marble tournaments and marble museums. This book has just about everything you'd ever want

You can play marbles almost anywhere.

to know about marbles. In fact, the only thing this book doesn't talk about is losing your . . . well, you know what I mean.

Why marbles? Because people love marbles. Don't believe it? Try showing anyone the marbles that came with this book. See if he or she can keep from picking them up, rolling them around or getting down on the floor and playing with them.

Marbles are fun. Some folks like to collect them. Just ask James Ridpath of Drexel Hill, Pennsylvania. He has over 160 thousand marbles in his collection. A serious collector pays hundreds of dollars for an old, hand-made marble. People have played marbles for thousands of years. The ancient Romans played marbles. Thomas Jefferson played marbles.

Mark Twain's Tom Sawyer played marbles. The Native Americans played marbles for hundreds of years before the Europeans came to America.

Thomas Jefferson played marbles.

A game of marbles is called Ohajiki in Japan.

Today, marbles are played around the world, in Europe, in South America, in Africa and in Asia. In China, in the emperor's palace, they played a marble game called Ishihajiki. This game is still played in Japan today, where it's called Ohajiki, but nowadays it's played with flat pieces of plastic instead of marbles.

In this book, you can learn some of the same marble games that folks have been playing for hundreds of years. These games have been passed down, from big kids to little kids, in neighborhoods, parks and playgrounds for years and years.

Some marble games take skill, and some are just silly. You can play for "keepsies" and try to win all your friends' marbles (try to not lose all your friends) or for "fair" and give them back after the game.

Either way, you can play marbles just about any-where—in a school yard, on the side-

Draw the playing lines with chalk if you play on asphalt.

walk, or on the kitchen floor. That's one of the great things about marbles—all you need is a smooth, flat playing surface and marbles! You can carry marbles around in your pocket, collect them and trade them with your friends. You can make up new games or change the rules of the old ones.

There are so many great things about marbles, you'd have to be crazy not to like them. In fact, if you said you didn't like them, people would say you'd lost your . . ..well, you get the point.

Many players have a favorite marble.

CHAPTER 1

Marbles Through The Ages

How long have people been playing marbles? Probably since there were people. It's easy to imagine some Ice Age cave man or woman sitting down after a hard day of being chased by saber-toothed tigers, taking out a bunch of pebbles and knocking them around the cave floor. After all, the Ice Age lasted 100,000 years, which is a long time to be cooped up in a cave. Marbles probably came in pretty handy.

But we don't have any proof that Ice Age people used marbles. The oldest known objects that might be marbles are small clay balls found in the tombs of ancient Egypt.

Small clay balls have been found in burial mounds of early Native Americans. These are almost 2,000 years old. Other small clay marbles have been found in Aztec ruins. We can't be sure if these were used as toys. But at least we know the Aztecs had marbles.

We do know for a fact that the ancient Romans played marbles. Well, actually they played marble games, but they used polished nuts as marbles.

By the time of the Middle Ages, marbles and marble games were widespread throughout Europe. Early marble games, played with clay or stone marbles, were probably more like bowling or the game of bocci than today's game of marbles. Shakespeare mentions a game called "cherry pits," which was probably played with polished stones (or maybe even real cherry pits). And glass blowers in the city of Venice made small glass balls as early as the 900 A.D.

In 1815, the earliest known book about marbles was published in

Kids used to use polished stones to play marbles.

England. It included several games that are still played today, like Archboard and Ring Taw. (You can find the rules for these games in this book). Marbles at that time were made of clay, china or glass, but the most popular for games were those made of polished stone, including some made of real marble. In fact, it was around this time that marbles became known as marbles. Marbles made of agate (with the nickname aggies) became the favorite of marbles players in Europe and the United States.

European settlers brought their marble games with them to America. Thomas Jefferson played and collected marbles. And Abraham Lincoln is said to have been a great marbles player. He played a game called Old Bowler.

Marbles were played across the United States from the streets of old New York to the frontier. In the book Tom Sawyer, Tom gets 12 marbles as part of his payment for allowing his friends to white-

Abraham Lincoln played marbles.

wash his aunt's fence.

Around 1890, there appeared the first machine-made glass marbles. These were made first in Germany and then in the United States. Back then, kids played a game called Conqueror. The object of the game was to see if you could break your opponent's marble with a really hard shot. Today some of those early machine-made marbles are worth hundreds of dollars. No one plays Conqueror with them now.

The first National Marbles Tournament was held in Philadelphia in 1922 and was sponsored by Macy's Department Store. A tournament has been held every year since, with the exception of two years during World War II. In the tournament's second year the runner-up was Babe Ruth. No, not that Babe Ruth. A girl

Both boys and girls can excel at marbles.

whose name was Babe Ruth came in second that year. This started a legend that the baseball great Babe Ruth was a marbles champ. Not true. He may have been the Sultan of Swat, but it was the other Babe Ruth who was the Queen of Marbles.

Speaking of queens, in the 1950s there was a real aristocrat who was a marbles champion. Her name was Lady Norah Docker. She made headlines by winning a charity marbles tournament in England. At that time it wasn't considered proper for a "lady" to be seen wearing pants, so Lady Docker had to knuckle down in a full-length evening dress. They did give her a golden cushion to kneel on, however.

The 1950s also saw two new marbles crazes sweep the United States. The first was the cat's eye marble.

This new type of glass marble was invented in Japan, and it almost sank the U.S. marbles industry. It took almost four years for American marbles makers to figure out how make glass marbles with the colored swirl inside, and by that time Americans had bought millions of the Japanese cat's eyes.

A cat's eye marble.

Around the same time, believe it or not, Americans decided to start cooking their marbles. Cooking glass marbles makes them crack inside without falling apart. People liked the designs the cracks made and used the marbles as decorations in jewelry and clothing.

But the biggest event in the history of marbles wasn't to come until the late 1960s. It was only then, with the

coming of space flight, that astro-
nauts discovered what marble players
had known for centuries. Not only are
marbles played around the world,
but in the words of
astronaut Neil
Armstrong, the
Earth is nothing
but a "big blue
marble." Maybe
that's why marbles
have stayed around
so long. Maybe those

*The earth looks like a
big blue marble.*

little glass balls remind us of our
planet shooting through space like
an aggie coming off the flick of a
cosmic thumb.

Okay, maybe not. Maybe it's just
a great game. But it gives you something to think about the next time you
get down on the floor to shoot a
game of marbles.

Ten Other Uses For Marbles

Marbles aren't used just in games.
Here are some other uses for marbles.

1. In pinball machines
2. As reflectors in road signs
3. As spawning beds in fish hatcheries
4. As agitators in aerosol cans
5. In vases for flower arrangements
6. As ball bearings
7. In oil filters
8. To prepare printing plates
9. To spin glass fibers
10. As rollers to slide coffins into crypts

Marbles can keep your flowers standing tall.

CHAPTER 2

Marble Lingo

I f you're going to be a marble shooter, then you should learn to talk like one. This not only makes the game more fun, it totally confuses most adults when you say things like "Don't plunk that snooger" or "How many mibs did you get?"

Here are a few handy words of marbles-player lingo:

Aggie A real aggie is made out of agate, a mineral. When machine-made aggies started being made in the 1800s, it changed the game of marbles. Machine-made aggies were harder and made better shooters. Today an aggie is one of the prizes given to the winners of the National Marbles Tournament.

Alley Short for alabaster, it's a marble made of real marble or a glass marble that looks as if it's made of real marble.

Bombsies When you try to drop your marble onto another marble.

Bombsies

Bumboozer A very large marble.

Cat's eye A clear glass marble with a twist of color inside.

Cat's Eye

Clearie Any clear glass marble of any color.

Comic strip A machine-made marble with a picture of a comic strip character on it.

Commoney An antique clay marble. The name comes from the word common.

Comic Strip

Corkscrew A glass marble with two or more spirals of color covering its surface.

Dubs When two or more marbles are hit out of the ring in one shot.

End of the day An antique hand-blown glass marble made from bits of leftover glass when the glassmaker's real work was over for the day.

For fair The opposite of keepsies. When you play for fair, everyone gets their marbles back at the end of the game.

Fudging Lifting your hand off the ground before shooting.

Glassy Any marble made of glass.

Handspan The distance from the

end of your thumb to the end of your pinkie, with your fingers stretched out. Used as a measurement in many games.

Handspan

Histing Lifting your hand off the ground before shooting.

Hunching Moving over the line while shooting.

Immie An immitation agate, made of glass.

Keepsies When you play "keepsies," you keep all the marbles you win in a game.

Kimmie Any target marble in a game.

Knuckle down The accepted way to shoot a marble in most games. At least one knuckle of your shooting hand, usually the first, must be on the ground while shooting.

Knuckling down means you have to have at least one knuckle down.

Lagging Rolling your marble toward a line or target to see who goes first.

*Mibs are any
target in a game.*

Lofting Making the shooter fly off the ground.

Mibs Long ago, it meant a clay marble. Now it means any target marble in a game.

Mibster A marbles player.

Milkie A solid white marble.

Onionskin A type of antique swirl marble that is completely covered with spirals of color.

Peewee A very small marble.

Plunking Making your shooter bounce or jump so that it hits the kimmie on the fly.

Puree Any solid-color, clear marble, no bubbles or imperfections.

Scrumpy knuckled A term to describe someone who hists.

Histing means your knuckle comes off the ground.

Slag A machine-made glass marble made to look as if it's made of agate or some other stone.

Snooger In the game of Ringer, a snooger is a target marble that has been knocked out of position but is still in the ring. Riding a snooger means hitting a snooger out while sending your shooter closer to the center of the ring.

Span or Spanner   The distance between your outstretched thumb and little finger. A handspan.

Steelie   A steel ball bearing used as a marble. Steelies make good shooters, but they can crack glass marbles.

Sulfide   An antique marble with a small sculpture inside.

Swirl   A glass marble with a spiral of color inside or on the surface.

Sulfide

Taw   A shooter. Some folks have a special taw that is larger than a regular marble.

A player holds a taw.

Tournament rules state that a taw may not be bigger than 3/4 inch across or smaller than 1/2 inch.

Taw line   Line from where you shoot your taw at the targets, kimmies or mibs.

A player draws a taw line with chalk.

CHAPTER 3

Buckle Down and Knuckle Down

How to Play

There are as many different ways to play marbles as there are types of marbles. There are even more names for marble games because a lot of games have different names, depending on where they're played. For example, the game Old Bowler is also known (with slightly different rules) as Skelly, Milkie and Spangy.

How to Shoot A Marble

If you're playing a friendly game of marbles (and I hope all your marble games are friendly, even if you're playing keepsies) you can shoot your taw any old way you want. But if you ever want to play with serious marbles players, or play in a marbles tournament, you're going to have to knuckle down.

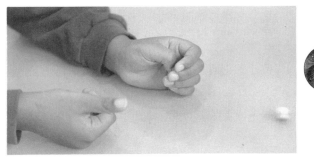

One knuckle should always be in contact with the ground when knuckling down.

Knuckling down means you shoot with at least one knuckle of your shooting hand touching the ground, usually the knuckle of your index finger.

To knuckle down correctly, get down on your hands and knees, and place your shooting hand on the ground, palm up. Place your shooter between your index and middle fingers, with your thumb curled behind it. Curl your fingers back, take aim and flick the shooter with your thumb.

If you've never done this before, it feels awkward at first. You may have to do it a few times just to get the marble to travel a few inches. And if the marble slips out before you have a chance to shoot, don't worry—this happens even to experienced marble shooters.

The marble should pop out of your hand and hit the ground, then roll toward the target. You may want it to go farther through the air, depending on the game and the shot you want to make. Some players get skilled at "plunking" or "hitting a line drive— the shooter flies through the air and hits the target without hitting the ground first. This takes a lot of skill.

Most players have a favorite shooter they use every time they play. Larger marbles make good shooters, but in most tournaments you're not allowed to use one that's bigger than 3/4 inch in diameter.

Marbles come in different sizes. Bigger ones make good shooters.

When you knuckle down, you're not allowed to lift your hand from the ground while shooting. Like everything in marbles, this error has at least four names. It's called hunching, fudging, scrumpy knuckling or histing, depending on where you are and with whom you're playing.

Lifting your knuckle off the ground while shooting is called hunching, fudging, scrumpy knuckling or histing.

Histing comes from the word heisting, as in "There was a jewelry heist the other night." Heisting probably

With practice, you can learn to put a backspin on your taw.

comes from hoisting. They all mean lifting, and whatever you want to call it, don't do it.

Really good marbles players can direct their shots like pool players with a cue stick. They line up their shots like a pool player or a golfer about to putt. They also have follow through—they allow their thumb to keep moving after flicking the shooter.

A good marble shooter can put backspin on a shooter. You do this by putting pressure on your shooter with your index finger as it leaves your hand. If your shooter has some spin on it, it will "stick," or stay in one place, after it hits another marble. This is a big advantage in some games. But learning to put backspin on a marble takes a lot of practice.

"Don't worry about backspin when you start," advises Gene Mason, the Director of the National Marbles Tournament. "Just work on shooting that marble out with a flick of your thumb."

Remember, marbles is a game of accuracy. What counts is not how hard you shoot but how well you can hit a target. If you want to get good at it, you have to play. Just don't play keepsies until you've played for a while, unless your family owns a marble factory.

Lagging

Lagging is the way marbles players decide who goes first in a game. Of course, there are other ways, like letting the littlest kid go first or going in alphabetical order or shouting, "They're my marbles so I'm going to go first or I'm going to take them all home!"

I recommend lagging.

You need two lines, a lag line and a shooting line. In tournament play, where Ringer is played, the lag line is drawn so that it touches the top of the Ringer circle and the shooting line is 10 feet away.

All the players line up behind the shooting line and roll or shoot one marble toward the lag line. Most people roll or bowl the marble. You

Players take turns shooting from behind the lag line.

do this by holding it in your hand and letting it go like a tiny bowling ball. The player whose marble is closest to the lag line goes first.

In tournament play, there's a board about a foot behind the lag line and if your marble hits it, you're disqualified. If you want to play this way, you can draw a second line a foot behind your lag line.

Where to Play

For centuries, marbles has been played in the dirt, which is probably one of the reasons kids liked to play. Nowadays, marbles is played just about anywhere—the dirt, the schoolyard, the sidewalk, the carpet, the kitchen . . .

If you're playing outside in the dirt, you can draw the playing lines right into the dirt. If you're playing on a hard surface like asphalt or concrete, use chalk. If you play inside on the floor or on a carpet, try making the lines with a thin string or thread.

The National Marbles Tournament is played on covered concrete. To get the same action, you can play on asphalt, concrete, a linoleum floor or any smooth surface, including hard-packed dirt. Of course, the games that involve digging a hole have to be played on dirt.

If you're paying on asphalt, use chalk to draw playing lines.

If you're playing on dirt, you can draw playing lines right into the dirt.

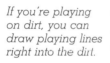

String can be used as a playing line when playing on carpet.

The Games

Here are the rules for over 50 different games of marbles. You may find a game you know by a different name, or rules that are different from the ones you play by. That's part of the fun of marbles. You can always make up your own rules and your own games. You can even name your game after yourself. Maybe that's how Skelly, Milkie and Spangy got started.

Feel free to bend the rules and play your own way. If the taw line is too far away for you, move it up until you find a place where it feels comfortable to shoot from.

Ringer:
The Tournament Game

Ringer is the official game played at the National Marbles Tournament every June. Although the rules were not set down until 1922, Ringer comes from one of the oldest marble games, Ring Taw.

Ringer is played in a ring or circle that's 10 feet in diameter. Thirteen marbles are set up in the shape of a cross with the center of the cross in the center of the ring. The marbles in each arm of the cross are spaced 3 inches apart. The aim of the game is to hit the kimmies out of the ring without letting your shooter go outside.

Players decide who goes first by lagging. The player who wins the lag

In Ringer, the marbles are set up in the shape ▶
of a cross.

places his or her shooter anywhere outside the ring, knuckles down and shoots. Then you follow these rules. If you knock a kimmie out, you get to keep it.

If your shooter is still in the ring, you can shoot again from wherever your shooter has stopped.

Your turn is over if your shooter has left the ring. Pick up your shooter and keep any kimmies you have won. If you miss completely or don't knock a kimmie out of the ring, you pick up your shooter and your turn is over.

Any kimmies left in the ring are fair targets.

In a two-player game, the first player to hit 7 kimmies out wins. If more than two are playing, then the player with the most marbles at the end wins.

• •

The National Marbles Tournament

Every year since 1922, kids from around the country have headed for the National Marbles Tournament to display their lagging, knuckling down and other marble skills.

For many years now, the competition has been held in June in Wildwood, New Jersey. It's open only to kids 14 years old and under. The competition goes on for four days, and there are boys' and girls' divisions. In 1995, the champion in each division won a $2,000 scholarship along with a trophy and other prizes. See page 177 for information on how to enter.

• • • • • • • • • • • • • • • • • • • •

In 1941, there were five district marbles champs competing at the National Marbles Tournament in Wildwood, New Jersey.

Ring Taw

This game has been played in Britain for at least 150 years and probably much longer.

Draw a small ring 2 or 3 feet across. Each player puts the same number of marbles (5-10) into the ring.

Six feet from the edge of the circle, draw a taw line. (If you're good shooters, you can draw your taw line 10 feet from the circle.) The aim of the game is to hit the marbles out of the ring, without leaving your shooter inside.

The first player knuckles down at the taw line and shoots at the mibs in the ring.

If you knock any marbles out of the ring, you keep them. If your

 Ring Taw is one of the oldest marble games.

shooter leaves the ring, you line up at the taw line and shoot again.

If you hit a marble out, but your shooter stays in the ring, your shooter becomes a target just like the others. (In Britain they say it is "fat.") But you can use any marble you've hit out of the ring as a shooter and go on with your turn.

Any time you shoot and don't hit a marble out, you lose your turn. If your shooter has left the ring, you get to keep it. If it has stopped in the ring, you lose it. Then it's the next player's turn.

If you have no more marbles to shoot, you're out of the game.

The game ends when all the marbles are hit out of the ring. Whoever has won the most marbles wins.

Ring Taw II

In this version, players draw a small ring and place the same number of marbles inside. There is no taw line.

The aim of this game, as in Ring Taw, is to hit the marbles out of the ring without leaving your shooter inside. Players knuckle down anywhere outside the circle to take their shots.

All the other rules are the same as in Ring Taw.

An easier version of Ring Taw can be played without a taw line.

● ●

Marbles Champion:
David McGee

It took David McGee four trips to Wildwood, New Jersey, before he won the boys' division of the National Marbles Tournament. 1993 was his last chance because he was 14. The next year he'd be too old to compete. David had another reason to be nervous. His coach, Walter Lease, who'd been with him every other year, was, sick and in the hospital back in Pittsburgh. But David didn't let the pressure get to him. He dedicated his tournament to his coach, knuckled down and went on to win.

David first became interested in marbles in grade school when they had a schoolwide tournament.

"That was the first time I'd ever heard of marbles," he says. "I tried it and it turned out I was pretty good.

At that tournament David met Walter Lease, who was on the committee for the national tournament.

● ●

Soon David was practicing every day.

"I liked that it was a game where you depended on yourself, whether you won or lost depended only on what you did. "

After winning at Wildwood, David went on to play other marbles games. He tried his hand at Rolley Hole and also competed in the Mason Cup, which is for players who are too old for the Wildwood tournament. He's also passing on the skills he learned from Walter Lease by becoming a coach for a younger marbles player.

David still considers himself a marbles player. And he's always finding new people who haven't heard of the game.

"That's what I like about marbles," he says. "Everyone asks you how to play. It's fun to tell them about it."

Potsie

This game is played almost exactly like Ringer, but with one big difference — the winner gets to keep all the marbles that were in the ring to start with.

Each player puts an equal number of marbles in the ring. Set them up in a cross, as in Ringer.

Players take turns knuckling down from anywhere outside the ring. Like Ringer, your shooter has to end up inside the ring or you lose your turn. Unlike Ringer, if you knock a kimmie out and your shooter leaves the ring, you do not get to keep the kimmie. You put the kimmie back in the cross, pick up your shooter and lose your turn.

The first player to win more marbles than he put in at the start wins
the game. And if you're playing for
keepsies, he also wins everyone else's
marbles.

Potsie, like Ringer, starts out with the marbles set up in the shape of a cross.

Poison Ring

In this game, each player puts four marbles into the center of a ring. Lag to see who goes first.

Each player takes a turn shooting from anywhere outside the ring. If you knock a mib out with your shot and your shooter ends up outside the ring, you keep the marble and pick up your shooter. Your turn is over.

If you miss, or if your shooter stays inside the ring, you pick up your shooter and your turn is over.

The game continues until all the targets have been knocked out.

In Poison Ring, players shoot from outside the ring, trying to knock out mibs.

Poison Ring II

This game is similar to Poison Ring. Draw a ring, and each player puts four marbles inside. The players take turns knuckling down and shooting from anywhere outside the ring. As in Poison Ring, if you knock a mib out and your shooter ends up outside the ring, you keep the marble and pick up your shooter. Your turn is over.

If you miss, or if your shooter stays inside the ring, you pick up your shooter and your turn is over.

All the rules are the same as Poison Ring except one: If your shooter ends up inside the ring, it stays there and becomes a new mib.

String of Beads

This is another version of Poison Ring. Players draw a ring, and each player places the same number of marbles inside the ring in a circle shape. Each player knuckles down and shoots from anywhere outside the circle.

The rules are the same as for Poison Ring.

Marbles are arranged in a circle shape in String of Beads.

The outer circle in Double Ring Taw is the taw line.

Double Ring Taw

In this version of Ring Taw, you draw one ring and another ring inside it. Players put 5 marbles inside the smaller ring. Players shoot from anywhere outside the big circle, not from a taw line.

If you hit a mib out and your shooter leaves the ring, you keep the mib and shoot again from wherever your taw has stopped.

If you don't hit a mib out on your shot, your taw stays on the ground. You lose your turn.

Players can shoot at your taw. If it gets hit, you must pay that player one marble.

The game ends when all the mibs have been hit out of the smaller ring. The player with the most marbles wins.

The inner circle in this game is called the pound and the outer circle is called the bar.

Increase Pound

This game is similar to Double Ring Taw. Draw two rings, one inside the other. The inner circle is called the pound, the outer circle the bar. Each player puts five marbles in the pound. Each player knuckles down and shoots from anywhere outside the bar.

If you hit a mib out and your shooter leaves the ring, you keep the mib and your turn is over.

If you don't hit a mib out on your shot, your taw stays on the ground. You lose your turn.

Players can shoot at your taw. If it is hit, you must pay that player one marble.

The game ends when all the mibs have been hit out of the pound. The player with the most marbles wins.

Forts

This ring game is played with four rings drawn inside one another. The smallest should be about 2 feet across, the next is 4 feet across, the third is 6 feet across and the fourth is 8 feet across.

At the start, each player puts three marbles in the center ring, two in the next ring and one in the third ring. The outside ring is empty.

On your first shot, you shoot from anywhere outside the biggest circle. Only marbles in the third circle are fair targets. If you hit one out into the fourth circle, you get to keep it. You leave your shooter where it has stopped and play it from that spot on your next turn.

If you don't hit a mib out, you pay one marble into the third circle. Then it's the next player's turn.

When all the marbles have been hit out of the third circle, you shoot at the targets in the second circle and try to hit them into the third circle. Now if you hit a mib out, you get to keep it and you get a second turn.

When the second circle is empty, you shoot for the inner circle. Now you can shoot three times in a row, as long as you hit a marble out each time.

The game ends when the inner circle is empty. The player with the most marbles wins.

Forts is played with four rings drawn inside one another.

Forts II

This game is the same as Forts with a twist that makes it a lot harder.

The four rings are set up the same way and the marbles are arranged the same way. Players knuckle down and shoot from anywhere outside the fourth circle, trying to knock out the marbles in the same way as in Forts.

In this game you can shoot at another player's taw. You don't collect it, but you can knock it away from the targets, making the game more difficult.

Forts II is also played with four rings.

Tinsley Green: Britain's Best

The oldest marbles tournament in the world may be the one held every spring at Tinsley Green, England. Legend has it that the game has been played there every year on Good Friday since sometime in the 1500s when two men in love with the same woman challenged each other to a game of marbles.

The game is played similar to Ringer, except in the opening rounds it's played with forty-nine marbles in the ring, not thirteen. The shooter is called the "tolley. " The game is played on a layer of sand over concrete.

The tournament is organized by the very serious-sounding British Marble Control Board. Although it started as a British tournament, there are often teams there from other countries, including the United States.

Archboard

This game is from England and is one of the oldest known marble games.

To play, you need a shoe box. Cut four or five square doors in the edge along one side. Write a number over each door. Each number is the amount of points you score for getting a marble through the door. You can pick any numbers you want, but you might be upset if you're not the one to score 1,964 for one shot. Put the box down and draw a shooting line 5 or 6 feet away.

Decide on the number of shots each player will take, then take turns shooting for the doors. Each time you get through one, you score that number of points. After each shot you pick up your shooter. The player with the most points at the end wins.

◄ *You need a shoebox with numbers and cut-out doors to play Archboard.*

Bridgeboard

This is another version of Archboard. You can use the same shoebox as in Archboard. Put the box down and draw a shooting line 5 or 6 feet away.

Decide on the number of shots each player will take, then take turns shooting for the doors.

If you miss a shot, your shooter stays where it is.

If your shooter goes through a door, you get to pick up as many marbles as the number over that door.

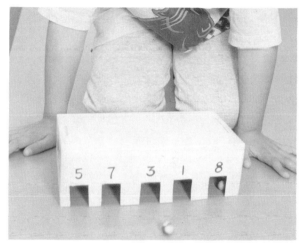

Bridgeboard is another version of Archboard.

Golf

This game is called Golf, but it's like Archboard without the arches. In fact the only way it's like golf is that it has holes. Kids used to play this game on manhole covers in the street using the designs on the covers as holes. Anyway, this is how you play:

Dig a row of holes in the ground in a straight line. Give each hole a

For Golf, you'll need to dig a row of holes.

Each hole in Golf must be numbered.

number between 1 and 10. Draw a shooting line about 10 feet from the holes. Players take turns shooting or rolling their marbles toward the holes.

If you miss a hole, your shooter stays where it is.

If you sink a hole, you pick up as many marbles on the ground as the number for that hole.

Poison

If you're playing on dirt, dig a shallow hole about 6 inches across and 1 inch deep. Then draw a taw line 3 to 5 feet from the ring.

In this game, being "poison" is good.

The first player shoots from behind the line and tries to get his or her shooter into the ring.

If you miss, you pick up your shooter and lose your turn. The next player shoots.

If your shooter goes into the ring, you become "poison." Leave your shooter where it is. The next player tries to get into the

The distance from the end of your thumb to the end of your pinkie is a hand span.

ring. From now on, you can collect any shooter that comes within a handspan of the edge of the ring.

If another player gets into the ring, then he or she gets a chance to knock you out. If she does, then you must give her all the marbles you've won so far and she becomes poison. If all the players take a turn and no one knocks out the poison player, then the poison player has won the game.

Capture

In England this game is called Plum Pudding or Picking Plums. Whatever you call it, it's a very simple game that's good for beginners.

Draw two straight lines about 3 feet apart.

Each player puts four marbles on a line. These are the targets, or kimmies.

Take turns shooting from behind the other line. If you knock a kimmie off the line, you get to keep it and you shoot again.

If you miss, pick up your shooter. Keep shooting until all the marbles are gone.

The player with the most marbles at the end wins the game.

In Capture, the kimmies are all lined up on one line. ▶

Dobblers

You play Dobblers just like Capture with one difference. Start by drawing two lines 3 feet apart. The players each line up four marbles on a line and take turns shooting from behind the other line.

The difference is if you miss a shot, your shooter stays on the ground and becomes a kimmie.

If another player hits your shooter, you must add a marble to the targets on the line.

Keep shooting until all the marbles are gone. The player with the most marbles at the end wins the game.

◀ *A player concentrates on the kimmies.*

One Step

Another version of Capture is called One Step. It begins the same way.

Draw two straight lines about 3 feet apart. The players each line up four marbles on one line.

Instead of shooting at the targets on the line, you stand behind the other line, hold your shooter over the kimmies at shoulder height, and try to drop your shooter on the kimmies. This is called "bombsies."

If you knock a kimmie off the line, you get to keep it and you shoot again.

If you miss, pick up your shooter. Keep taking turns until all the marbles are gone.

The player with the most marbles at the end wins the game.

A player uses bombsies to knock a kimmie off the line ▶ in One Step.

Football

There's still one more version of Capture. It's called Football.

On the ground, draw a football shape about 4 feet from pointy end to pointy end. Then down the middle of the football draw a line. Draw a shooting line a few steps away.

Each player puts two marbles on the line in the football. Then the players take turns shooting from behind the taw line, and trying to knock a marble out of the football.

If the kimmie doesn't leave the football, it gets put back on the line. It doesn't matter where your shooter ends up.

You get only one shot each turn. Keep shooting until all the kimmies are gone.

Whoever has the most marbles at the end wins the game.

◄ *Football is played on a football shape.*

Rebound

Draw a line about 2 feet from a wall. This is your target line. Each player places one marble on the line.

Draw another line, 3 feet farther from the wall. This is your shooting line.

Each player knuckles down at the shooting line and tries to hit a kimmie off the target line. But the shooter has to bounce off the wall first.
If you miss, your shooter stays on the ground.

If your shooter hits a kimmie off the line, you get all the marbles on the ground and the game starts over. If no player knocks a kimmie off the line on the rebound, the game continues. But in the second round, everyone shoots from wherever their shooter has stopped. In this round, you collect only the kimmies you knock off the line.

You keep shooting until you miss. Then it's the next player's turn.

The winner is the player with the most marbles at the end.

When playing Rebound, players aim for the wall first before hitting a kimmie off the line.

Hit and Span

Draw a shooting line on the ground.

The first player rolls his or her marble away from the shooting line. This is now the target, or jack.

The next player knuckles down on the shooting line and tries to hit the jack. If the shooter hits the jack or comes within a handspan of it, then the shooter collects both marbles. The next player in line rolls out a marble for a new jack.

If the shooter misses, then the taw becomes the new jack. The first marble stays on the ground. The first player to hit the jack or come within a handspan wins all the marbles that are on the ground.

Before you play Hit and Span, you have to draw a taw line.

Bossout

Here's a version of Hit and Span with bombsies.

The first player drops a marble in the middle of the playing area. This becomes the target.

The other players walk off about 10 feet from the target and draw their own shooting lines.

When you shoot, you try to hit the target or come within a handspan of it. If you do, then collect both marbles and the game starts over, with the next player in line dropping the target.

If you miss, then both marbles stay on the ground. The next player shoots at the first target.

Whoever hits the target first collects all the marbles on the ground. Then the game starts over.

If all the players shoot and no one

hits the target, measure off a circle one giant step away from the target. If your marble is outside the circle, you get to pick it up. If your marble is in the circle, you get to try bombsies. Pick up your marble, hold it at shoulder height above the target and try to hit the target with it.

The first player to hit the target this way gets to collect all the marbles in the circle.

A player knuckles down.

Bounce About

This very simple game is similar to Bossout. Instead of shooting, you roll or throw your marble at the target.

Draw a line on the ground. The first player rolls a marble any distance away from line. The second player tries to hit it. If she does, she keeps it and then she rolls out a new target. If she misses, then her marble stays on the ground and the third player tries for either marble.

If a player hits more than one marble on a single throw he keeps them all. If all players miss, then they pick up their marbles and the game is over.

◀ *Players roll or throw their taws in Bounce About.*

Chasies

In Chasies, you first draw a snake-like course on the ground, with two curving parallel lines running anywhere from 10 to 30 feet long.

The first player stands at the start of the course and rolls a marble so that it lands in between the two lines. The second player shoots at the first player's marble. If she hits it, she wins it and the game starts over. If she misses, then she stands where her marble has stopped and rolls it farther down the course. Now it's the first player's turn to try to hit her target.

The game continues until one player hits a marble or the players reach the end of the course.

Players play inside a snake-like parallel lined course ▶ in Chasies.

Bombers

Here's another game in which you drop or throw your marble instead of shooting it. It's a version of Hit and Span for two players.

Players throw the shooters in bombers.

Start behind a shooting line. The first player throws a marble along the ground. This becomes the target, or mib.

The second player tries to hit the mib. He or she can shoot, throw or roll the shooter at the target.

If the shooter hits the mib, he or she collects it. Then the first player has to drop a new marble in the same spot.

The second player then tries to hit the new target bombsies style, by dropping a marble from shoulder height.

After the second player tries bombsies, the game starts over, but the players switch. Now the second player throws out the target and the first player tries to hit it.

Straight-Arm Bombers

You play this game exactly the same way as Bombers, except you have to hold your arm straight out when dropping the marble.

A player bombs a kimmie.

Black Snake

This game is like golf with marbles. You need to play on dirt so that you can make holes. Set up your holes like a golf course. The holes should be 4 or 5 feet apart. You can make as many holes as you want. Draw a start line 4 or 5 feet from the first hole. Lag to see who goes first.

The first player shoots for the first hole. The object is to sink the shooter in the hole. Or you can allow spanners—if a player gets within a handspan, it counts as a hole.

If the first player sinks a hole (or spans into one) then he places his shooter next to the hole and tries for the next one. He can keep shooting as long as he keeps sinking holes.

◀ *Players try to roll their shooters into holes in Black Snake.*

When the shooter misses a hole, then it stays wherever it stopped and the next player shoots.

When a player sinks the last hole, he becomes a "black snake." He then uses his turn to shoot at the marbles of other players. If he hits the marble of another player, the player is out of the game. But if his marble falls into one of the holes, he is out of the game.

The game continues until everyone is either out or has finished the course.

Sidewalk Black Snake

If you're playing on the sidewalk, you can still play Black Snake. Instead of holes, just use objects as targets, such as books or cans.

To "sink a hole," you have to hit an

object with your marble. Then you can go again, playing from wherever your marble stopped.

Black Snake can be played on the sidewalk as well.

Die Shot

This game gives you the chance to win a few marbles with one shot — if you're playing keepsies. Besides marbles you'll need a die.

The first player has to balance the die on top of a marble. Push the marble into the dirt to stabilize it. If you're playing on asphalt, play with a marble that has been ground down on one side so it stays put while the die sits on top. This is your target.

Draw a shooting line 5 or 6 feet away from the target. The other players take turns shooting at the target.

If a player misses, then the first player collects that marble. If a player hits, then the first player has to pay the shooter the number of marbles showing on the top of the die. Then that player sets up the die on the target and the game begins again.

The hardest part of Die Shot is balancing the die on the marble.

Pyramid

They say the ancient Egyptians played marbles, so maybe Pyramid is what they played.
The first player is the pyramid builder. He or she stacks thirteen marbles in a pyramid shape.

Draw a circle around the pyramid about 18 inches away from it, and draw a

A player stacks 13 marbles in a pyramid shape.

Players collect marbles that are shot out of the circle.

shooting line a few feet away from the circle.

The next player takes a shot at the pyramid. If he or she misses, then the pyramid builder collects the shooter. The next player takes a shot.

If a player hits the pyramid, he or she collects any marbles that roll out of the circle. Then he or she gets to be the pyramid builder.

Rolley Hole

Rolley Hole is a very old game that has been passed down for generations. It probably comes from England, where a version is called Three Hole.

Rolley Hole is played on an area of tightly packed dirt called a marble "yard." You need three holes in a straight line, each about 2 inches across and no more than 1 inch deep. In a tournament, the holes are 10 feet apart. But you can make them 8 or six feet apart—or even closer.

You can play Rolley Hole with any number of players, but it's most often played in teams—two teams of two players each. To decide who goes first, one player from each team lags.

A Rolley Hole game is played in three rounds and each team tries to sink their marbles into the holes four times, in this order: middle hole, top hole, middle hole, bottom hole. (You decide which one is top and which is bottom). That makes twelve holes in a game.

You do not have to knuckle down, you can roll or toss your marble. You can also "span" into a hole. If your marble comes within a handspan of the hole, you're allowed to place it in the hole on your next turn. When you do make a hole, you "span" out and take a turn toward the next hole.

You can also shoot at other player's marbles to knock them as far away as you can.

· ·

Rolley Hole Country

Travel to Monroe County, Kentucky, and Clay County, Tennessee, and you'll have no trouble finding marble players. Nearly everywhere you go, you'll find folks playing a marbles game called Rolley Hole. And I don't mean just kids. The game is taken very seriously by adults who play it in marble yards in parks, outside factories and in backyards.

Bob Fulcher works for the Tennessee State Department of Parks and helps organize the annual Rolley Hole Tournament.

"People all over the South used to play marbles—adults and kids," Fulcher says. "I don't know why people kept on playing here. It's strange to me that they stopped doing it everywhere else."

Rolley Hole players play with marbles made of flint, not glass, and a lot of players make their own. Every year on the second weekend after Labor Day, teams gather at Standing Stone State Park in Hilham, Tennessee, for the annual tournament. Players of any age can compete, and often

· ·

11- and 12-year-olds face off against grownups.

Rolley Hole isn't played much or even well known outside this small area, but that's starting to change.

In 1991 six Rolley Holers went to Tinsley Green, the annual British marbles tournament. The players, all grown men from Kentucky and Tennessee, beat teams from Britain, France and the Netherlands to become world champions. How'd they do it? With a lot of skill and one secret weapon—they brought along a suitcase full of dirt from their home town, which they worked into their hands before every shot.

American sharp-shooters face opponents at Tinsley Green, 1991.

Amanda Burns and her coach.

Marbles Champion: Amanda Burns

Amanda Burns of Moss, Tennessee, was 12 years old when she won the girls' championship at the National Marbles Tournament in Wildwood, New Jersey. That was in 1993, and she'd been playing marbles for three years.

"My step-granddad has a marble yard next to his house," she explains. "He plays Rolley Hole. When I moved to Tennessee I started watching him, and sometimes he'd let me play."

Amanda thought playing marbles looked hard, but she also thought it was a great challenge. She used to play every day during the summer. Pretty soon she was playing in school and county tournaments. By 1992 she was playing in the national tournament.

"I never figured I'd go that far," she remembers. "That first year at Wildwood I didn't make it to the finals. "

Amanda kept playing, though, and when she went back to Wildwood the next year, she was in first place throughout the whole tournament.

After she won, Amanda received a $2,000 scholarship and some other prizes. Her name was in all the local papers (she has a scrapbook of all the newspaper clippings). She was interviewed on TV.

Wildwood champions have to retire from playing at the tournament after their victory, but Amanda has helped coach and referee at the tournament for the past three years.

What does it take to be a marbles champ? "You have to play a lot," advises Amanda, "and learn how to put spin on your shot so it sticks. "

And she has a special word of advice for girls.

"Girls can be just as good as boys," she says. "You just have to be ready to try hard."

Alleys

The rules for Alleys are very simple.

One player places a single target marble on the ground. (Usually it's a special marble—it has to be to get the other players to risk their marbles for it.)

The other players knuckle down at a shooting line 10 feet away. If a player misses, the owner of the target collects the shooter's marble. If a player hits the target, he or she collects the target. Then that player puts down a target and the game starts over.

A player knuckles down.

Players have to risk a special marble in Alleys. If another player hits it, she keeps it.

Spangy

This game for five players is known by several names but Spangy seems to be the most popular.

First draw a 1-foot-wide square. Each player puts in a marble, one at each corner of the square and the fifth in the center.

A player draws the square playing field.

Draw a shooting line 10 feet from the square.

The players take turns try-ing to shoot a mib out of the square. If you hit one out, you collect it and your shooter and go again.

A player tries to span two marbles together.

If your shooter stops within a hand-span of a target, then you may try to "span" the marbles. Place your thumb beside one marble. Place the little finger of the same hand beside the other and try to knock them together. If you do, then you keep them both and shoot again from the shooting line.

If you miss and your shooter stays inside the square, then you lose it and it becomes a target. If you miss and your shooter ends up outside the square, you collect it and lose your turn.

The game ends when all the targets have been hit out of the square. The player who has the most marbles wins the game.

Skelly

This is a version of Spangy. To play, you start the same way. You draw a square, and each player puts in a marble, one at each corner of the square and one right in the center. You draw a shooting line 10 feet from the square.

The players take turns trying to shoot a kimmie out of the square. But in this version, if you hit one out, you collect it only if it leaves the square "on the fly." It is very hard to play. You have to practice plunking to make those mibs jump out of the square.

Skelly with Bombsies

In this version of Skelly, the rules are the same except that you drop or throw your shooter at the targets.

A player knuckles down to a game of Skelly.

Old Bowler

This game, another version of Spangy, is the game that Abraham Lincoln is supposed to have played. As in Spangy a marble is placed in each corner of a square. A fifth is placed in the center of the square. This target is called the Old Bowler.

Players shoot from behind a shooting line and try to knock the targets out of the box. But you may not hit the Old Bowler until you've knocked out the other four targets. If you hit it, even by mistake, you're out of the game.

Otherwise, the rules are the same as for Spangy.

The marble in the center is the Old Bowler.

Big Tennessee

To play Big Tennessee, you need extra-large marbles—as big as golf balls. If you don't live in Clay County, Tennessee, you probably won't be able to find any, so you can use golf balls. These targets are called "dollars."

To play, draw a square and place the dollars in each corner, the middle of each side and one in the middle of the square. The dollars can be 2 or 3 feet apart.

You play with two teams of two players each. The aim of the game is to win all nine dollars by knocking them out of the square with your shooter. As you might guess, it takes a few shots with a regular marble to move those big dollars.

Each player shoots from behind a

shooting line a few feet away. If you hit a dollar out of the square, you keep it and go again. If you don't, leave your shooter where it stopped.

The next player can try to hit a dollar out or can aim at any shooters. If you knock out a shooter, you go again. If your shooter is knocked out, you must put back one of the dollars you have won. You can put it back anywhere on the square.

The first team to win all nine dollars wins the game.

The kimmies are called dollars in Big Tennessee.

A player tries to drop her taw on a mib.

Bounce Eye

In Italy this game is called Nucis, which means "nuts." This is probably because the game was first played with real nuts.

In Bounce Eye, you don't shoot or even roll your marble. Instead, you play bombsies—you try to drop your shooter onto the target marbles.

You need a ring that is anywhere from 3 to 5 feet across. Each player puts three marbles into the ring.

The first player stands anywhere outside the ring. You hold a shooter out at shoulder height and try to drop it onto one of the targets.

If you knock a marble out of the circle, you get to keep it and go again. If not, then you collect your shooter and the next player goes.

The game continues until all the target marbles are gone.

Stand-up Megs

This is a version of Bounce Eye. In this game, the rules are the same, but players have to stand 2 feet from the edge of the circle and throw their shooters at the targets.

A player throws her shooter at a target.

Dropsies

This is another version of Bounce Eye. In this game you draw a square on the ground instead of a circle. The players each put three marbles into the ring and take turns dropping their shooters on the mibs.

If you knock a marble out of the square and your shooter stays inside, you keep it and go again. If not, you collect your shooter and the next player goes.

The game continues until all the target marbles are gone.

This version of Bounce Eye is played on a square field.

Hit the Spot

Believe it or not, some people call this game Lose Your Marbles. (I didn't say it, they did.)

You play this game on dirt. Dig a small, shallow hole. Draw a shooting line about 10 feet from the hole. One player puts a marble in the hole.

All players line up behind the shooting line and take turns tossing or rolling marbles at the target in the hole. If you miss, you leave your marble on the ground.

The first player to hit the target three times wins the target and all the marbles on the ground.

Then the game begins again, with a new player putting the target marble in the hole. The game continues until all the players have put a target in the hole.

Players take turns aiming at the marble in the hole ▶
in Hit the Spot.

Hundreds

For this game, you need just two players with one marble each. Make a small hole if you're playing on dirt, or draw a small circle on your playing surface. Back up 10 feet or more and draw a shooting line on the ground.

It doesn't matter who goes first in this game—both players get one try to shoot their marble into the target. If both players make it, they pick up their marbles and shoot again.

If only one player makes the target, she scores 10 points and goes again. She can keep shooting as long as she makes the target. Each hit scores 10 points. If she misses, then she picks up her marble and the other player gets to try. The game continues until one player scores 100 points.

◀ *The first player to make 100 points wins in Hundreds.*

Newark Killer

Legend has it that this game was invented by kids somewhere in New Jersey.

To play, you need a sneaker lace. Some players will use a shoe lace, but that's not traditional. Velcro is a definite no-no.

Tie the lace in a loop. Place the loop on the ground. Draw a shooting line about 10 feet away.

Each player takes ten marbles and takes turns trying to shoot or roll them into the loop. You have to keep count of how many of your marbles end up in the loop. If someone knocks one of your marbles out of the loop, you lose a point. If someone knocks one of your marbles in, it counts as a point.

When everyone has shot all their marbles, the player with the most in the loop wins. Then comes the "killer" part of this game.

The winner gets to shoot at any marbles on the ground that are outside the loop. If she hits a marble, she collects it and goes again from wherever her shooter stopped. As soon as she misses, the game is over.

You'll need a shoelace to play Newark Killer.

A player tries for Tic-Tac-Toe

Tic-Tac-Toe

This game is exactly what you think it is. Like tic-tac-toe, this is a game for two players. First draw a tic-tac-toe board on the ground, then draw a shooting line 6 or 7 feet away.

Players take turns shooting for the tic-tac-toe squares. If your marble lands in an empty square, leave it there. If you miss the board or your marble stops in a square that already has a marble in it, pick up your marble. Either way, your turn is over.

The first player to get three squares in a row or on the diagonal wins, just like in tic-tac-toe. But there's one more rule: You can knock the other player's marbles out of a square. If you do, you leave your marble in the square and the other player must pick up his or her marble.

Knuckle Box

Here's a simple game played in a square.
Draw a square about 2 feet on each side. Each player puts four marbles into the square.

Players take turns knuckling down and shooting from a handspan anywhere outside the square.

If you knock a mib out and your shooter leaves the box, you get to keep the mib and shoot again.

If your shooter stays in the box, you can keep the mib you have knocked out, but you lose your shooter and your turn. Your shooter is now a fair target for other players.

The player with the most marbles at the end of the game wins.

The object of Knuckle Box is to knock as many mibs as you can out of the square.

Poison Pot

This difficult game is played in two parts. In the first part of the game, all the players compete to see who will become poison.

Part I

Whoever gets to be poison gets a chance to win everyone else's marbles. This is definitely a game you play for "keepsies."

First dig a shallow hole, about 6 inches across. If you're not playing on dirt, draw a 6-inch circle. Around this draw a bigger ring, maybe 3 or 4 feet across. The hole or small circle is called the poison pot. Each player drops a marble into it at the start of the game. Each player also places three marbles in the outer ring a few inches out from the poison pot. These are the kimmies or targets.

Poison Pot is played for "keepsies."

To see who goes first, lag to the edge of the outer circle from 10 feet away.

The first player knuckles down anywhere along the outer ring and tries to hit a kimmie out of the ring. (The marbles in the poison pot are

In Poison Pot Part I, you keep shooting until you miss.

not targets.) If you hit a kimmie out of the ring and your shooter leaves the ring, you keep the kimmie. If your shooter stays in the ring or you miss, then you must pay a two-marble penalty into the poison pot. Then the next player goes.

If you win a marble, then you can shoot again. You keep on shooting until you have won ten marbles — as long as you don't miss or leave your shooter in the ring. If you do miss or your shooter stays in the ring on any shot, then you have to put all the marbles you've won into the poison pot and lose your turn.

If all the target marbles are gone before a player has won ten marbles, then the game is over and you divide up the marbles and start over.

But if someone wins ten marbles, he or she shouts "Poison!" and the second part of the game begins.

Part II

The poison player divides up the marbles he has won among the other players. The other players also pick up any of their target marbles that are left in the ring.

The poison player shoots to keep.

Poison then picks up all the marbles in the poison pot and places them in a circle around the pot. The player who would have gone next takes all his marbles and places them around the outer ring. The poison player then shoots his poison marbles at the other player's marbles. If he hits one out of the ring, he keeps it.

As long as poison keeps hitting the marbles out, he keeps shooting. But as soon as he misses, the other player can pick up the rest of his marbles. Then the next player lays down his or her marbles and poison gets a chance to win them. As you can see, whoever is poison gets a chance to win everyone's marbles.

Make sure you play this game with very good friends who don't mind losing their you-know-whats.

Players shoot for a prize marble target in Immie.

Immie

This game is for kids who really like to collect marbles and are willing to take a chance to get one that's really special. The rules are very simple.

One player offers a valuable or special marble as a prize. She puts it in the middle of the playing field and draws a shooting line about 10 feet away. The other players line up, knuckle down and try to hit the prize. If they hit it, they keep it. If they miss, the owner of the prize gets to keep their shooters. Once the prize is won or all the players have taken a shot, then someone else gets to offer a prize.

Rockies

Rockies is another game in which one of the players puts up a prize. You play it like Immies, but in this game the prize is usually a dozen marbles — maybe even a whole bag.

Of course, it has to be really hard

to win that prize, which is why Rockies is played on a side-walk with a lot of cracks, bumps and holes. Each player knuckles down 10 feet away and tries to hit the prize in one shot. It should be really hard to do but not impossible.

The prize is so special in Rockies that it should be ▶ really hard to win it.

Potty

This is another hole game, if you're playing on dirt. If you're playing on asphalt or concrete, you can use a cup or even a shoe as a target.

If you're playing on a hard surface, you can use a cup as a target.

If you're playing on dirt, dig a shallow hole about 1 foot across and less than 1 inch deep (not really a hole, just a circle-shaped dip in the ground.) This is your pot. Next draw a shooting line anywhere from 6 to 10 feet away.

Lag from the shooting line to the pot to see who goes first. The closest to the pot without going in wins the lag.

Each player shoots and tries to sink her marble in the pot.

A player tries to sink a marble in the pot.

If a player sinks her marble in the first round, then every other player pays her one marble and the game starts over. If the player misses the pot, then she must leave her marble on the ground where it stopped.

If no player sinks her marble on the first round, the game continues until someone does. Then that player gets to collect all the marbles that are within a handspan of the pot. All the other marbles on the ground are given back to their owners. (In this game, if you're going to miss, miss by a lot!)

But wait a minute—before she can collect those marbles around the pot, the next player in line gets three chances to hit the marble of the player in the pot. (If you're playing with a shoe or a cup, then the next player tries to hit the marble in the pot by dropping on it bombsie style.)

If she can do it, then she gets to collect the marbles within a handspan.

Either way, the game starts over.

Boxies

The name of this game comes in handy because it reminds you of the equipment you'll need—a shoebox.

This game is really simple. Put the shoebox on its side. Back off about 10 feet and draw a shooting line. Each player takes a turn rolling a marble toward the box. The aim is to roll a marble into the box. (It helps if the open side of the box is facing you.)

Sound easy? It would be except if a marble bounces out of the box, it doesn't count. The first player to get a marble to stay in the box wins the game.

You'll need a shoebox to play Boxies.

Puggy

You can play this game on dirt with a shallow hole about 6 inches across. If you're playing on concrete, you can draw a circle on the ground.

Draw a large ring around the hole, maybe 8 feet across. Every player puts an equal number of marbles in the ring, but not in the center hole.

Players try knocking mibs into the hole in Puggy.

Players take turns knuckling down around the edge of the ring, trying to knock the targets into the hole. If you knock one in, you get to keep it and shoot again from outside the ring. But if your shooter goes into the hole, you don't get to keep the target and you lose your turn.

If you're not playing on dirt, the game is a little harder because the target has to roll into the small circle and stay there.

A player concentrates on his taw.

Long Taw

This is a game for two players. Draw a line on the ground about 6 feet long. Each player places one marble at each end of the line. Then draw a shooting line about 6 feet from the first line.

The first player gets behind the shooting line and shoots at either one of the marbles. If he hits it, he picks it up and shoots at the second one from wherever his shooter has stopped. If he hits the second, he picks

The second player can shoot for the first players shooter.

that up and the game starts over, with the other player going first in the next round.

If the first player misses on either try, then he must leave his shooter wherever it has stopped. Now the second player shoots. The rules are the same as for the first player, except that the second player can also shoot at the first player's shooter. If she hits it, then she wins everything on the ground.

If the second player misses any shot, then her shooter also stays on the ground. Now the first player goes again and now he can shoot for the second player's shooter. Play continues until both of the target marbles are hit.

Eggs in the Bush

This is not like the other games in this book because you don't shoot or roll a marble to play. Instead, it's a guessing game played with marbles.

Whoever goes hides any number of marbles in his hand. The other players have to guess how many there are. If any player guesses the

How many?

right numbers then she wins all the marbles. But if she guesses wrong, then she must pay the player with the hidden marbles the difference between the guess and the number of hidden marbles. For example, if you guess five and there are three marbles, you must pay that player two marbles. If you guess three and there are five, you also pay the player two marbles.

If you guess right, you win all the marbles.

Odds or Evens

Another variation of Eggs in the Bush is called Odds or Evens. As you can tell from the name, in this game you must guess whether the player is hiding an odd or an even number of marbles. If you guess right, the player hiding the marbles must pay you one marble. If you're wrong, you pay him one marble.

In this game, a player passes whether there is an odd or even number of marbles hidden.

CHAPTER 5

Aggies, Cat's Eyes and Bumblebees:

Marble Collecting

There's something about marbles that makes people want to pick them up and play with them. Maybe it's the colors or the shape or the way they feel in your hand. Not only are the colors and designs beautiful, the names are great, too: cat's eyes, flames, there are hundreds of them. Sometimes the name tells you what the marble is made of (aggies, steelies.) Sometimes they describe what they look like (swirls, clearies).

There are allies, commonies, immies, slags and sulfides. And these are just a few of the different types of marbles that are out there waiting to be collected.

Swirlie

Some are very hard to find at your local toy store, while others are made and sold by the tens of thousands. But you don't need special marbles to play, and if you collect them, liking a marble is special enough.

New glass marbles, the kind you'll find in a toy store, are mainly solid color, clear or cat's eyes. Bumblebees, Cub Scouts, Popeyes and the rest stopped being manufactured sometime in the 1950s. But that doesn't stop some

Aggie

Clearie

people from trying to find as many of them as they can. These folks are known as marble collectors.

If your fingers twitch whenever you see a new type of marble, you're probably a marble collector. Marble collecting can creep up on you. After all, once you have more than one marble, you have a collection. A lot of collectors start out that way. They add a marble here and a marble there and before you know it, they have 160,000 marbles.

Galaxy

Strange as it may seem, the best marbles for playing are not the ones most collectors are interested in. Players usually want shooters made of stone, such as agate, or flint. But collectors usually want marbles that are rare or unusual. If a certain type of marble is

Bumblebee

Flame

hard to find, that makes them much more valuable. Antique marbles, hand-made glass marbles and machine-made marbles that are no longer being produced are all types sought after by collectors. A rare machine-made marble can be worth hundreds of dollars. And a set of glass agates from the 1930s, in the original box, could be worth a couple of thousand.

But don't start collecting with the idea that you're going to stumble onto a thousand-dollar marble. Those jackpots are few and far between, and that's why collectors are willing to pay so much for them. Most marble collectors start by just keeping marbles they like because of the color, design or size or because the swirls of red, yellow and green reminds them of the hat their Aunt Ethel used to wear.

Helen Mohr, the Marble Queen of Perry Hall,
Maryland has a huge collection of marbles.

• •

How A Marble Is Made

Here's a piece of good news for you: Not only are marbles fun, they're ecological, too. Most glass marbles are made from recycled glass. That means that soda bottle you save for recycling might come back to you one day as your favorite shooter.

Glass marbles are made of recycled glass.

Outside a marble factory you'll see huge mounds of clear broken glass, ready for a new life as marbles. The glass is broken into small pieces and then shoveled into large furnaces where it's heated to over 2000 degrees. To make solid-color marbles, different chemicals are added to the mix.

At that temperature, the glass melts into a kind of thick, syrupy goo. The molten glass, which is glowing red, is poured out of the furnace through a narrow tube. If the glass is going to become

• •

marbles with bits of color inside, like cat's eyes, then bits of color are pushed into the glass as it comes out.

Next, large shears cut off small hunks of the soft glass, which drop down between two large metal rollers. The rollers have grooves in them. The glass chunks fall into the grooves and the rollers form them into round balls. Now they're marbles.

The new marbles move down the grooves in the rollers. If color is going to be added to the outside of the marble, it's done now, before the glass cools. By the time the marbles get to the end of the rollers, they've cooled off. After that they're sorted, boxed and shipped, ready to be shot, plunked, lagged and dropped.

Marbles cool as they travel down the shoot.

Some collectors never pay more than a few cents for a marble. Instead of looking for antiques or one-of-a-kind marbles, many collectors look for marbles that appeal

to them. They might collect only red marbles or only peewees. Or only marbles that they think are pretty or unusual or cool.

Steelie

You definitely should not pay more than 25 cents for a marble until you know something about the types of marbles and what they are worth.

Where do you find marbles? Ask around. Your Aunt Ethel may have a few stashed in the attic. Other relatives, especially older ones, proba-

Swirl

bly played marbles when
they were kids. See if they
have any hidden away.
(You may have to challenge
them to a game before they'll

Cat's eye

give up their favorite shooter. I won-
der if Aunt Ethel has been practicing
lately?) Yard sales and flea markets
are another good place to find old
marbles. But again, don't
spend very much for a
marble until you really
know what you're doing.

A great place to see lots
of marbles and meet a lot of
serious collectors is a marble show.
One of the biggest is held every
spring in Amana, Iowa. There
are other yearly shows in
Columbus, Ohio, east-
ern Massachusetts and
Atlantic City, New

Comic

American Flag

Jersey. Admission to these shows is usually only a few dollars, and for that you get to see thousands and thousands of marbles of all types and sizes. The collectors who display their prized aggies and slags are usually glad to talk about their collections. But be prepared—some of those bits of glass have giant-sized price tags.

Of course, most people never get that serious about marble collecting. Since kids started playing with clay commoneys, marbles have always been an inexpensive way to have fun. Keep the fun part in mind when you're building your collection and you won't go wrong.

Some people are very serious about marble collecting.

· · · · · · · · · · · · · · · · · ·

The Marble Man: Everett Grist

Everett Grist is a name well known to marble collectors. He's written several books on the subject including Everett Grist's Machine Made & Contemporary Marbles, Everett Grist's Big Book of Marbles and Antique and Collectible Marbles.

Grist has these words of advice for beginning marble collectors.

"There are lots of interesting ways to collect marbles. One of the most interesting collections I have seen was put together by a woman named Helen Grainger of Mason, Michigan. She collected pairs of marbles. In each pair there would be a shooter-size 1-inch marble and a common 5/8-inch one. The two would be the same color or type except for the size.

"You can also collect by name. Kids and collectors have given marbles lots of interesting names. You can collect only a certain type of marble, or just one of each type.

"A lot of people call me with marbles they claim are unusual or rare. One guy called up and said he had a Santa Claus marble in amber glass. I'd

· · · · · · · · · · · · · · · · · ·

• • • • • • • • • • • • • • • • • •

never heard of one like that—usually they're in clear glass. He sent it to me and I told him it was worth $1600. He told me he'd bought it in a box full of marbles and that the whole box had cost him $2.

"But that sort of thing is very rare, almost like winning the lottery.

"For instance, I got another letter a few years back from a woman who said she'd bought a marble with a picture of Mickey Mouse on it and she thought it must be very rare since it wasn't in my book. The person who sold it to her said it was very old, and she'd paid fifteen or twenty dollars for it. But I had to write back and tell her that to the best of my knowledge, Mickey Mouse marbles weren't made until a few years ago.

"So don't concentrate so much on finding that pot of gold at the end of the rainbow. The enjoyment comes from searching for it but still being satisfied with the little odds and ends you find on the way.

"And the best way to get old marbles is if a kid keeps a marble until he's as old as I am. Then it's an old marble."

• • • • • • • • • • • • • • • • • •

Index of Games

Marbles Information:

Marbles Hall of Fame

In Wildwood, New Jersey, just a few blocks from the beach and the site of the National Marbles Tournament, is the National Marbles Hall of Fame, a room in the George F. Boyer Historical Museum. Just like halls of fame for other sports, this one has the names and photos of past champions along with historical photos and, of course, plenty of marbles. For more information, you can write to:

National Marbles Hall of Fame
Holly Beach Mall
3907 Pacific Avenue
Wildwood, New Jersey 08260
Telephone 609 523 0277

J. Will Disney-the 1937 Marbles Champ.

Tournament Information

To enter, you have to compete in a local tournament. If there's no tournament in your area, you might be able to talk a teacher or someone in your town's parks department into starting one. If you can get an adult interested, he or she can write to:

National Marbles Tournament
Director Gene Mason
810 Rayne Drive
Cumberland, MD 21502.

If you want to visit the annual Rolley Hole tournament, it's held every fall in Hilham, Tennessee. For the exact dates and other information, write to:

Rolley Hole Tournament
Standing Stone State Park
1674 Standing Stone Park Highway
Hilham TN 38568

Collector's Information

How do you find out more about marbles? If you're really serious, you might think about joining

The Marble Collector's Society of America
P.O. Box 222
Trumbull, Connecticut, 06611.

For $12 a year they will send you their quarterly newsletter, Marble Mania. They are a good source for price guide books about marble collecting and other resources.

If you're on the information superhighway you may be able to find other marble collectors on the Internet. For instance, America On Line has a marble collectors bulletin board in the Hobbies area.

Marbles
Picture Credits

Page 75: New York Public Library Picture Collection.

Page 115: Photo by Bob Fulcher.

Page 116: Photo by Bob Fulcher.

Page 170: Photo by Bob Fulcher.

Page 171: New York Public Library Picture Collection.

Page 180: Collection of Bob Fulcher.

Acknowledgments

Special thanks to all the mibsters who made this book possible:

Helen Mohr, the Marble Queen of Perry Hall, and her Perry Hall Mibsters: Anthony, Madelina, Kristen, Anne, Shaun, Nina, Michael, Kathy and Mike.

Mac Slover and his kids at the Charles Barret Recreation Center in Alexandria, Virginia: Kevin, Pierce, Todd and Leslie.

Lucky Elliot, Sheila Whiting and Tanya Hawkins and their kids at the Nannie J. Lee Recreation Center in Alexandria, Virginia: Danielle, Brittaney, Donta, Andre, Tabitha, Tysheea, Tamise, Tawanna and Xavier.

And thanks to Sophie.